Completely Loco

A new look at old railway

by
'Fishplate'

GW00374373

Silver Link Publishing Ltd

© 'Fishplate' 1991

First published in October 1991

British Library Cataloguing in Publication Data

Fishplate
Completely loco: a new look at old railway photographs.
I. Title
395. 0941

ISBN 0 947971 69 6

Silver Link Publishing Ltd
The Trundle
Ringstead Road
Great Addington
Kettering
Northamptonshire NN14 4BW

Typeset by G&M, Raunds, Northamptonshire
Printed and bound in Great Britain by
Woolnough Bookbinding Limited,
Irthlingborough, Northamptonshire

Cover illustrations
Front LNER Class 'A4' 4-6-2 No 60026 *Miles Beevor* at Ferryhill shed, Aberdeen, May 1965.
Back Brienz Rothorn Railway No 6 receives attention at Brienz in August 1975.

Publisher's Apology

Silver Link Publishing Ltd very much regret that due to circumstances beyond their control, and as a result of certain personal information injurious to the Publisher having fallen into the author's hands, they have no choice but to publish this book in its entirety. They are aware that this will cause distress to many readers, but felt that it was preferable to the alternative of trying to secure the return of certain negatives by depositing a quantity of unmarked bank-notes in a left luggage locker at Waterloo station.

The author of this book is — or, after you've read it, you may prefer to say *was* — a well-known and well-respected railway historian, whose name appears on books and numerous articles in the railway press. He is also the possessor of an extensive library of railway photographs, and here, we suspect, is where the trouble started. Most of us are content to concentrate on whether the loco is a 'D11/1' or a 'D11/2', whether it's the first and only time it appeared on the 11.54 newspaper empties in that particular livery, whether it was uniquely fitted with the Ravioli valve gear, and other matters of crucial importance to the hobby.

But for the poor individual whom we are obliged to call 'Fishplate', things began to go seriously awry, and he gradually became obsessed with what the people in the photographs were saying to each other — even what the *locomotives* were saying to each other. His wife and family — distraught, and understandably so — sought medical advice. A course of Working Time Tables and old Ian Allan 'ABCs' was prescribed to try and regulate the condition. But alas, it was too late.

'Fishplate' is now in hiding in the West Country, being cared for by sympathetic relatives. He gives rare press interviews, heavily disguised, which mostly consist of the poor fellow giggling hysterically at a photograph of a 'C14' at Oldham (Clegg Street), but apart from that he is seldom seen. Neighbours describe him as 'an ordinary, quiet sort of bloke' — 'as long as you don't mention "Howard of Effingham", of course,' one ruefully points out. 'Or the Easton Neston Mineral & Towcester, Roade & Olney Junction Railway,' adds another, from bitter experience, as they all nod knowingly.

So, can anything be done to help? Well, by buying this book you have contributed to the ongoing cost of medical attention, and have also helped the Publisher meet the ever-increasing cost of the monthly pay-offs to stave off disclosure of certain information. Further, the Publishers have been asked to make a donation to the W. Heath Robinson Foundation for the Rehabilitation of Those Inclined to be Silly about Railways.

However, laughter is the best medicine, they say, and I am sure we join with the author of this travesty in saying that if it gives you as much pleasure to read as it has given us to prepare, we will be very pleasantly surprised. . .

'Railway station? Yes, first left, then left again.'

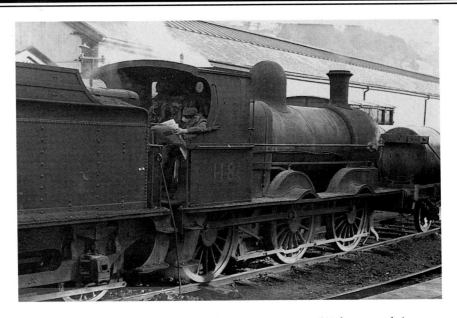

'It says here that railway productivity went up 15% last month.'

'Attention all Inchicore employees! Don't forget next Saturday's Bring & Buy Sale. . . '

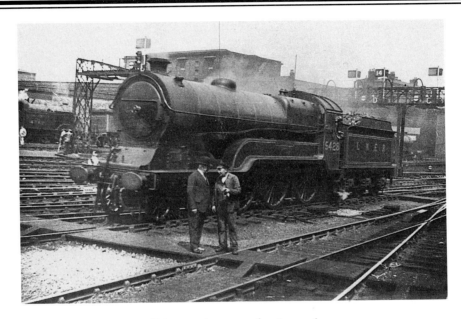

'It's a grating sort of noise. . .'

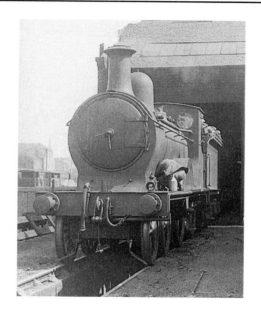

'Here, puss, puss, puss. . . '

'I wish your father wouldn't keep referring to this kind of thing as a "delightful family group". . .'

'I'm afraid that's the best I can get on Radio 3.'

'Albert, look – you can see the sea from here!'

'Please excuse Christopher from school today. He is not at all well. . . '

'I told him last week there was a bird's nest down there.'

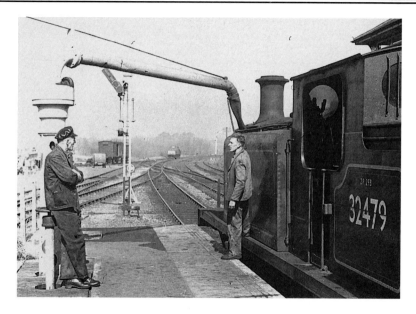

'No, my mum wanted me to be a ballet dancer.'

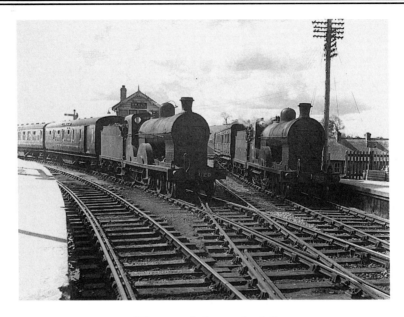

'I know – let's toss for it!'

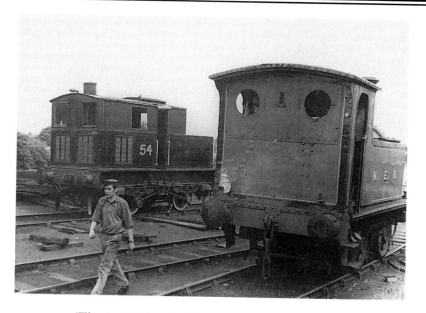

'That's it. If I can't drive steam, I'm not playing!'

'Go on, let me back in. I promise I won't call you that again. . . '

'D'you think we'll need umbrellas. . .?'

'Sorry, we've been told not to talk about it.'

'Never give up, that's me. I told you I'd find the cause of that squeak in the end.'

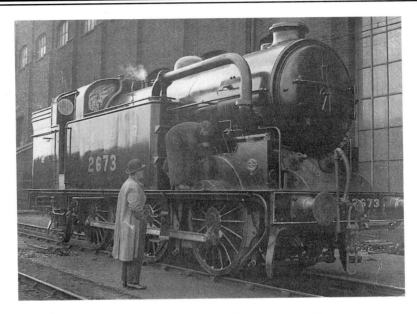

'You *still* think there's a bit missing. . .?'

'Do you ever get the feeling that there's more to life than driving that about all day. . . ?'

'And who's going to *make* me?'

'Maybe not – but it keeps the rain out. . . '

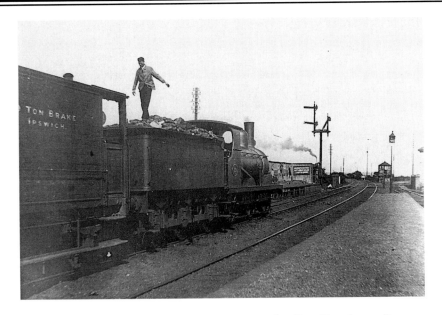

'Never mind the signal! Don't start yet, for Gawd's sake. . . !'

'They won't let him practise any other way.'

'I said, don't worry – we're always here in case you need us. . . '

'Right then, I'm off! Don't forget to lock up.'

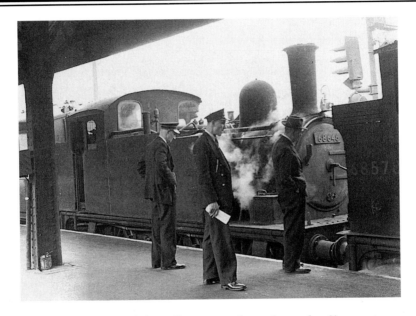

'So how did an alligator get down there, then?'

'On your marks, get set. . . !'

'Blimey! We had *three* on when we left Rovenden!'

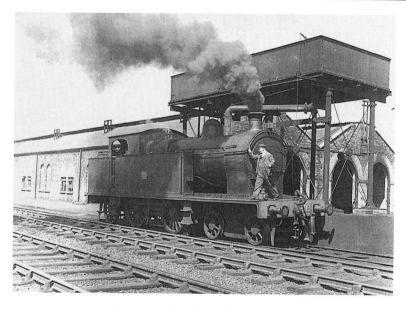

'Doing the Lambeth Wa-alk. . . ! '

Any moment now. . . !

'Right, one last chance! Are you coming out, or do I fetch the police?'

'Well, not straight away! You'd both have to become engine cleaners first.'

'Personally, I still prefer steam. . .'

'Oh, I like the flower vases, don't you, Arnold?'

'Geoffrey, stop teasing that train!'

'I hate spring cleaning. . .'

'Look what *I've* dug up with my little shovel!'

'No 1 Paint Shop comedians are heartily invited to a Laugh-In at the Foreman's office at 8 o'clock sharp, Monday morning.'

'Dunno. Must be some pop group we've never heard of.'

'They never learn, do they? Don't lean against that engine, I told him. . .'

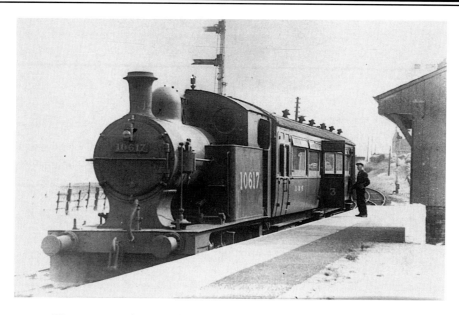

'I'm sorry, madam – I don't care if it *is* only a baby elephant. . . '

'This train doesn't move until we get luncheon vouchers.'

'Splendid! Once we get a few carriages we'll be away. . . '

'Hold it! I've spotted a rabbit.'

'I'm not quite sure why – we're just not speaking. . . '

'That reminds me, I must wash my hair tonight.'

'What d'you mean, Bob-a-Job Week. . . ?'

'Mmm, nice morning! I fancy I might just break a speed record or two today.'

'Now I don't want you two lads gallivanting about on the front when we get there, is that understood?'

'Aye, there was none of this dashing about when I was a lad. . . '

'Michael, Michael, ye'll be the death o' me! Where's the sense in me pushin', and you pullin'?'

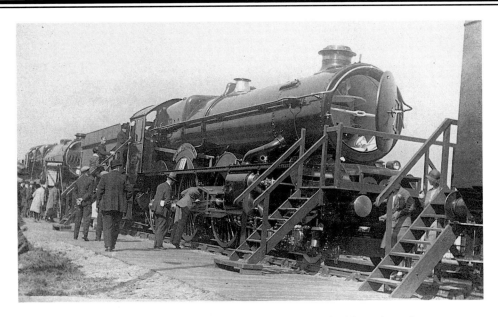

'You must admit it's a silly place to get your head stuck. . . '

'Look – no hands!'

'Just one last thing before ye go – are ye alright for spare wheels?'

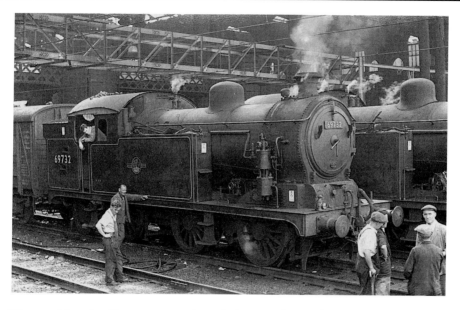

'He says blow the Roman excavations, he's got to be at Chingford for 5 o'clock.'

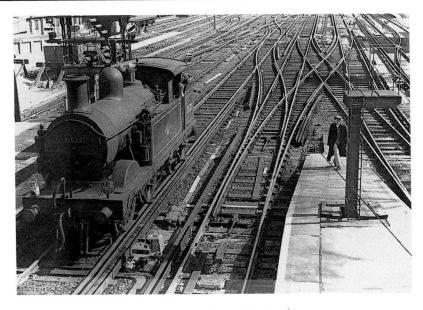

'Oh, and two packets of Polos. . . '

'As you know, I'm not one for gossip, but did you hear about the Shed Foreman. . .?'

The truth of the matter